The Qualities of Craftsmanship

By
Kent Carlos Everett

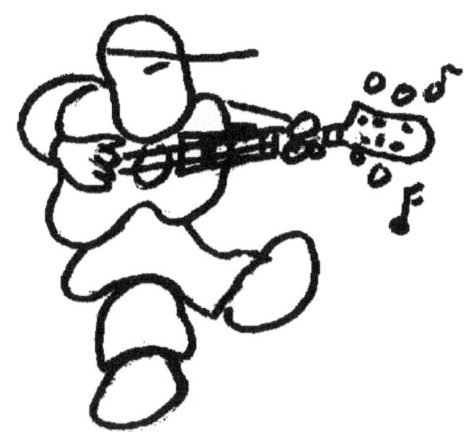

Introduction

I was pretty nervous sitting on that cold metal fold-out chair. But I was ready.

I had practiced Eric Clapton's version of Hideaway until I could do it in my sleep. I was well prepared.

I slid through the song with ease, and my teacher said, *"Wait right there."*

"Listen! You bent the string from the G to the A."

A tad defensively I said, *"Well, that is how the song goes."*

With a smile, *"No; it's not. Listen."*

He played back the live recording of Clapton.

By now, I knew every little part of that song by heart, I thought.

> *"Listen, ... here he does not quite make that bend. He is shooting for the A natural, but on this recording he falls a little short of the bend. It is actually just a little bit flat. If you want to sound like Clapton playing Hideaway, don't go all the way to the A."*

Well, that opened my ears.

I heard the song in a completely different way. I heard music in a completely different way. Now I listen not only to the vibrato but to the speed of the vibrato, not only to the individual notes but also to how the notes are approached.

In that instance, I learned to hear.

This is Craftsmanship.

My goal is to extend this same quality of teaching to my students. When they bring me a guitar to evaluate, or when I am teaching a guitar building class, I want to open the eyes, the ears, and the heart to the beauty of an excellent job.

Content

Note
I, of course, know many very talented female craftsmen. For simplicity through this book I use "he" and "craftsman", as is common in the English language, to refer to human beings, both male and female.

Also the principles demonstrated in this book can apply to a variety of work. Acoustic guitars are our vehicle, because they have been my life.

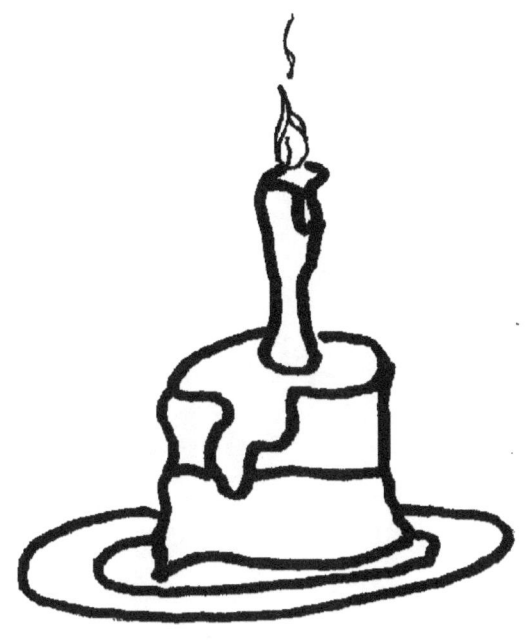

*For those of you who like to eat your dessert
first, go ahead and start with Part 2.*

*Part 1 is philosophy in practice.
It is the foundation for Part 2.*

*But if you just cannot wait, it will not kill you if you
simply start with the useful workshop
information found in Part 2.*

I will not hold it against you …

Your First Step

**In order to improve you need to learn to see, feel,
and hear things that you have not been able to before.**

Your first step on this journey, of improving your quality, is to see high quality workmanship up close and personal.

In order to appreciate and understand the details of finish work, miter joints, binding, interior cleanliness, neck fit, rosettes, neck pitch, fret work, aesthetic balance, weight, balance, and certainly tone and playability, you have to see the work in person.

Perhaps even more importantly, take the opportunity to watch it being done. When you see another human being performing what you yourself want to do, well… suddenly it all seems possible.

How can you get there if you do not know where you want to go?

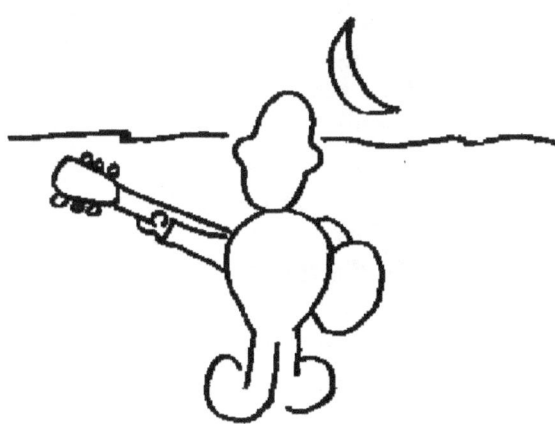

Have a look at your destination.

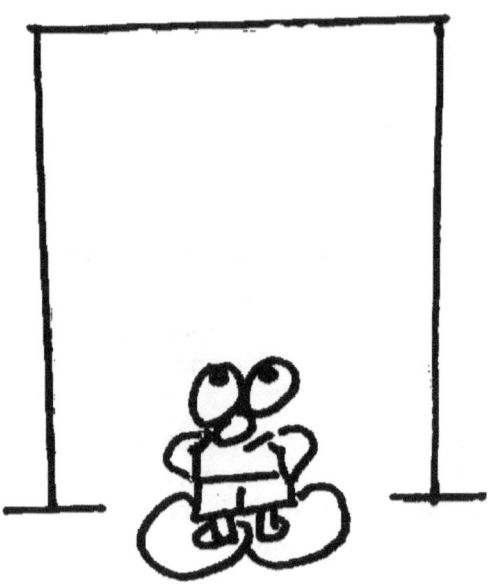

The High Jump

In High School while trying the high jump for the first time, someone might really enjoy jumping onto the soft landing pad. It's fun. Until the coach points out the bar, he would not really understand the point. Now with a little work, training, and time he might become the best high jumper at his school. Then arrives the first track meet where he sees the other guys jumping - a lot higher. So with more practice and help from the coach, he can grow to a competitive level. At this point he is feeling pretty good about himself with the stack of trophies and award metals adorning his bedroom – until he sees the Olympics.

"Holy cow! I did not even think that was possible!" Now he might be thinking, *"Well .. that guy is my size and weight. I train as hard as he does. If he can do it, why not me?"*

He now knows this will require a new level of commitment in terms of time, diet, training, and competitive level. But he has taken the first step.
He has seen "it" and has made the decision to pursue it.

Part 1 - The Qualities

Craftsmanship of Dexterity

The worker pushing the chisel through a piece of mahogany in order to make something beautiful is what I call Dexterity Craftsmanship. This type of craftsmanship has no safety net and relies one hundred percent on the skill of the craftsman himself. This "wild approach" is perhaps the most rewarding. Taking the time to sharpen your favorite chisel to the point that it is so sharp you dare not check it with your finger *(It is best to slice it through a piece of paper to see how cleanly it cuts),* then pushing it through the handsome piece of wood specifically selected for your piece … well it does not get any better than this. With no middleman, you are in direct contact with your objective. You watch the hidden sculpture slowly emerge from the beautiful piece of wood. Your experience will dictate the angle that the chisel travels through the wood and your immediate executive decisions will determine the outcome.

Wahoo. This is the good stuff.

Or not.

This can also be where the student gets frustrated and sometimes even hurt. Developing dexterity is of vital importance and, not unlike the high jump, it takes time, practice, coaching, and focus.

Here is the eye opener. Your outcome does not have to be completely reliant on Dexterity Craftsmanship. The quality of your work is a dance between several different aspects of workmanship.

This is good news for you as you grow into your potential.

Exercise 1

(You need only pencil and paper for this one. No ruler.)

Draw a straight line on the paper. Do this entirely by hand with no ruler or straight edge. Make your line approximately 12" long. Go slowly or quickly. Try horizontal and vertical. Left to right; right to left… try it all. Which combo works best?

Focus on making the line as straight as possible using nothing but your hand and the pencil. Simply use your natural hand control. Try a few times.

You just exercised **Dexterity Craftsmanship**.

**"All workmen using the workmanship of risk
(Dexterity Craftsmanship)
are constantly devising ways to limit the risk
by using such things as jigs and templates."
David Pye**

With Dexterity Craftsmanship the outcome of the work is determined 100% by the craftsman's "by hand" ability.

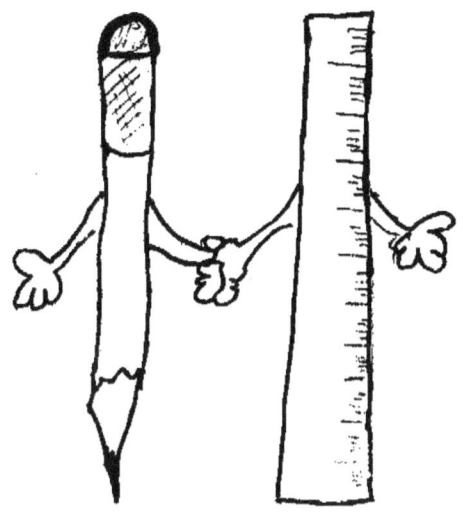

Craftsmanship of Control

Control is Dexterity's best friend.

In order to improve your chances of a pleasant outcome, let's add some **Control** to the mix. Unlike Dexterity Craftsmanship, Control Craftsmanship can be accomplished with tooling and often is safer.   Neither Dexterity nor Control Craftsmanship can live well without the other.

Exercise 2

(This time you will need paper, pencil and a straight edge.)

Draw another 12" line on the paper only this time use a straight edge. Compare it to the lines in exercise one. Easier? Better? Faster?   You just used **Control Craftsmanship**.
By adding jigs, templates, and even tooling, you can reduce your reliance on dexterity and improve your outcome.

Now really look at those lines. Do they get fatter and thinner as they travel across the page? Did the pencil hop?

In the drafting of yester-year, we had to learn to rotate the pencil in our hand as we drew. This not only kept the pencil sharp but also kept the lines an even thickness.

This example (although outdated) well exemplifies the use of both Control and Dexterity Craftsmanship together. It takes Dexterity to roll the pencil and maximize the use of Control – the ruler.

Keep in mind it also takes Dexterity to make the jig or to adjust it. Then once regulated, you will be able to execute your work with more Control.

**Control does not replace Dexterity but helps it.
They work together.**

Consider this:

You have two Sitka spruce steel string acoustic guitar tops.
You want to thickness them to become a soundboard
from a rough .180 to a smooth .110.

Thickness top 1 by hand using a sharp plane.
There is a lot of info on the web concerning planing a guitar top by
hand. It is not hard and could be an enjoyable evening. This one
evening of hand work will influence the rest of your guitar building
experience, … for many years to come.
Why not give it a try?

Thickness top 2 using a drum sander.
(Borrow one if you don't own one.) If you planed top 1 by hand, you
will now appreciate what the drum sander is doing for you. Wow!
How much easier and faster this is! And it is much more uniform.

After experiencing hand work with the first top, you now have a much
broader awareness for how the drum sander is serving you. You will
appreciate the tool, maybe for the first time. The complaining will
stop when the sander gives you a problem. You will have a deeper
awareness for what is happening to your guitar top as it goes through
the sander. It is that much easier.
The caveat is that by doing it entirely by tool, you never develop an
awareness for what the tool is doing to the wood.

By never doing this by hand, you would miss the
opportunity to have a personal connection with the work.

Is top 2 better than top 1?

Not necessarily.

Top 2 will be beautiful and even; yes.

No nicks, chips, or heavy scratches. You will gain control over the amount of wood you remove from the top. The drum sander process cannot get away from you as fast as the plane method can. Visually top 2 will be much better. You have experienced Control Craftsmanship in the form of the sander

Top 1 will be uneven.

You might not even be able to see it, but the plane hits hard and soft fiber as it travels across the wood at a 45 degree angle. It rides up and down on the wood in a minute manner. It scrapes the wood surface smooth - open grain - instead of packing dust into the wood pores like the sander. It is risky, exciting, and tactile. In a heart beat, it can leave you waving your arms around in your shop, swearing like a sailor, with a vicious chip in your top.

Is the end product better? In some ways yes and some no.

Top 1, the planed top, could be argued to be a more musical top. The uneven and open pores lend themselves to a freer and looser vibration. Being planed instead of homogenized via the sander, perhaps the top's flex follows more naturally the individual top's grain and fiber characteristics. I believe this is why many planed top Spanish guitars have a tonal character that is so alluring. They have the warmth and depth of tone that romantically pulls you in. Once you hear a great classical guitar, you can never not hear it.

What a fun topic for thought. Consider the hand carved f mandolin versus the CNC carved mandolin. Which do you think sounds better, has more personality - more power?

**Can you think of a way you can use both
Control and Dexterity Craftsmanship?**

I thickness my tops via drum sander and complete the last .010 by
hand using a scraper.
This gives me both control over the top thickness as well as the open
pores and uneven fibers of scraped wood.

Open yourself up to something new. Both processes. Perhaps you can
think of similar situations where both would come in handy.

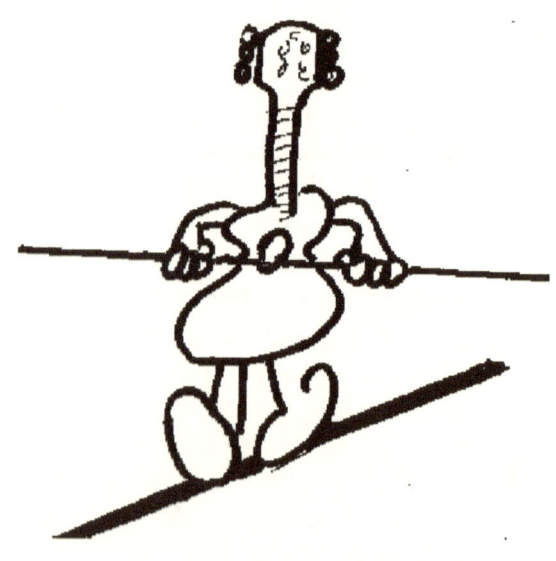

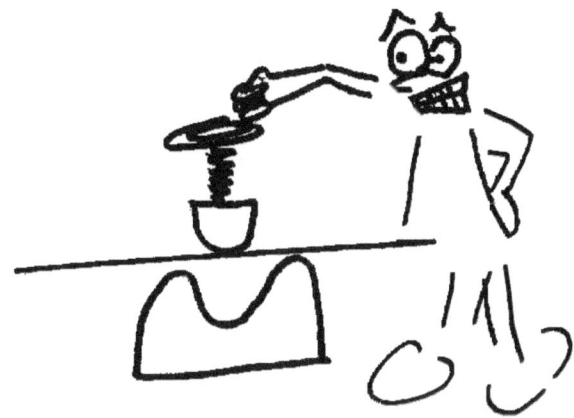

Example – Side bending

In my classes we experience this with a guitar side bending exercise. I want each student to feel the wood bend by hand over a hot pipe (Dexterity Craftsmanship). They need to feel the cells flexing in the wood as it stretches and sense the compression as it bends. Feel the heat coming off the pipe and the wood. Smell it and watch the steam. Get involved with what you are doing.

After each student has done this, the class moves to side bending using modern day techniques (Control Craftsmanship).
First we feel what is happening to the piece of wood in order to appreciate what the tool gives us.

By adding the tactile process to your knowledge base, you will find yourself with more confidence while using the jig technique. Now you will be able to feel the wood bending in the jig. You can use the tactile knowledge learned by dexterity and apply it to control. Your success ratio will go up, because you are **not** relying 100% on the jig.

**Add templates, jigs, and specialized tooling,
then watch your Control improve.**

**With your growing Dexterity,
you will enjoy watching your Quality improve.**

Craftsmanship of Process

**I teach that with each guitar completed,
we are actually building 3 things:**

**The <u>Workshop</u> ,
that supports the <u>Process</u>,
that builds the <u>Guitar</u>.**

With every instrument, if you keep all three things in mind,
you will gain Control.

Don't just get the instrument under string tension as fast as you can.
Stop and think about how it went. If you change the steps of the
process, will it go smoother? If you move this tool in your shop from
here to there, will it reduce time and energy in hauling material
around? If you detail this part now, will you have to detail it again
later in the process? *"Do I really need to wind this nut on this jig 25
times? Can I cut the thread shorter and save energy...?"* Think about
what you are doing and your shop layout will improve, then your
process and tooling will smooth out. The guitars will get better.

**Working on Process amps up Control and lowers
the need for Dexterity even further.**

How did they do it?

In the 1980s I worked in a high end guitar repair shop that was next to a great music store in Atlanta. All the local guitar heroes used to hang out there. I would often go over in the morning with paper, pencil and a cup of coffee to copy the outline of a guitar shape that I liked. I would sit there with my rulers and drafting paper making my own blueprints from "live" models. Sometimes I drew from the great guitars of the past and sometimes from an aesthetically pleasing newer model.

I remember those guys laughing at me, in a good natured way, when they saw me scoping out an inexpensive guitar from overseas. *"Well, I guess there sits American craftsmanship copying Asian ingenuity."*

They were right.

I was amazed at how clean those instruments looked especially for the price. I had to ask myself, "How did they do it?" I knew they were not putting the hours in on their finishes that I was, but look how nice the finish looks. I knew they were not spending the same hours sanding every little corner of the interior like I was, but look how clean the interior looks!

Later I started my own mini guitar production, and the fog began to lift. They did it by working on the Process.

I saw my own quality levels limited by Dexterity Craftsmanship improve with Control and Process. And I was able to reach my lofty goals with less effort. That changed something that was frustrating into something rewarding, and it will for you too.

Now after having built over 800 instruments, I build only a dozen or so annually. But I am still using these same principles learned from my solo production days. I am having fun. You do not have to be planning on setting up a factory to take advantage of this.

This is simply great information for everyone.

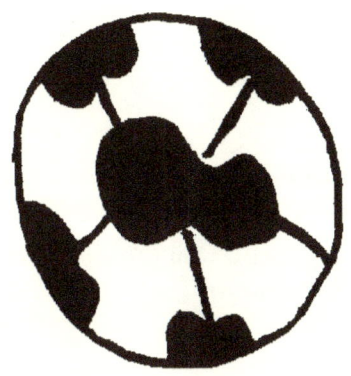

Example – Bend it like Everett

Let's return to the side bending example. If you buy a side bender, it has the potential to give you Control. If you follow the guidelines as to: how thick the wood should be, how wet, how hot, etc., you are following a Process. The Process that assists the Control.

Now, if you have bent some sides by hand, you will feel the wood bending in the side bender. Your awareness has been opened to what is happening to that piece of wood. With this knowledge you do not have to rely 100% on the Process (often set by someone you do not know, in a city far, far away…) and simply hope for the best. Now you are utilizing all three parts of craftsmanship: Dexterity Craftsmanship (your knowledge of wood bending, how it feels, and its limits), Control Craftsmanship (the clever side bender you built or bought), and Process Craftsmanship (The "How" guidelines: how thick, how wet, how hot, how long ...)

**With Control the outcome of the work is
pre-determined by the Process.**

**The Process helps Control.
Control helps Dexterity**

Exercise 3

(paper, pencil, straight edge)

This time, draw 2 straight lines,
One horizontal and one vertical.
They should intersect in the exact middle of the page.
Give it a try and do a good job.

When did you do what?

Did you sharpen the pencil before you began? Would it have been a
better end product if you did? Was your work area clean or was there
a little something under the paper messing up your line? Where did
you put those lines? Did you pay attention to the basic requirement of
having an intersection in the middle of the page? Did you "trial and
error" your approach or did you measure and give yourself a little
guide mark on the paper's edge? Did you erase your guide marks?
Did you find the center of the page via diagonals ...?

Or did you simply do a fast crummy job?
Your choices. Your final product.

Perhaps do it again.

With a little thought you can add **Process Craftsmanship**
and become more powerful.

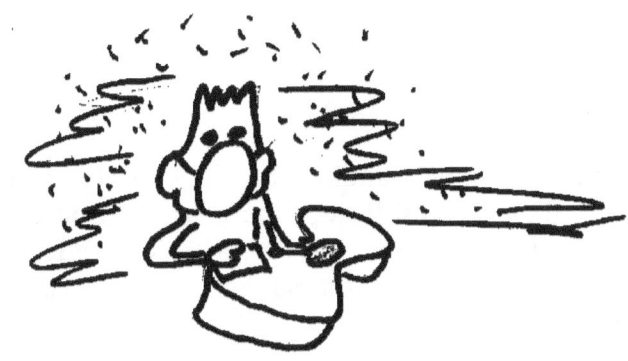

The Sander

Luke takes his guitar body out of the mold, and how exciting! The pieces are starting to look like a guitar. Then he proudly sands the sides smooth as a baby's bottom to 400 grit sandpaper. It's absolutely beautiful.
It takes a lot of time, but it is worth it. This is his masterpiece after all. He is taking pride in his work, and he should. This is a big deal - building a guitar.
Later he comes back and cuts the ledges for the binding to fit.
Damn it!
The binding jig marred those beautiful sides. The bit's bearing actually scored the sides a little. Oh well, he sands them again taking more time and at this point his hands are getting a bit tired. So let's glue in the binding.
Damn it!
After the binding is dry, he sees some glue squeeze out that needs to be taken care of or perhaps the binding is a little proud in a spot or two. He sands it once again.
Damn it! … On and on it goes. And each time the sides do not get sanded quite as well as the time before…

Lots of misery here.

Let's avoid the familiar one step forward and one step backwards routine. You can make your guitar in a fun progressive manner - if you think about **Process Craftsmanship**.

In the above example, sanding the sides to 80 grit to get them even for the binding jig to follow is the goal. Then after cutting and installing the binding, he could have scraped or sanded the sides to 100 or 120 grit in order to level the binding and take care of any large scratches (80 grit).

After cutting the neck joint and fitting the neck (pre-gluing) he could then sand the sides to 180 grit. And finally after the guitar has been completed, after all the fret banging has taken place, after all the gluing (except the bridge), after all the Dexterity has been completed … now is the time in the Process to finally do the pre-finish 220 grit sanding. (320 or 400 can cause you problems with fill adhesion – depending on materials…)

A thoughtful **Process** can save a lot of effort,
and the end product is actually better.

Next time you get the "Damn Its" stop and pay attention to what is happening. You will be able to save yourself a lot of grief.

*"Workmanship is the exercise of care
plus judgment, plus dexterity."*

David Pye
The Nature and Art of Workmanship

Craftsmanship of Design

Design and Process are first cousins
and work together to assist Control.

Exercise 4

(Paper, pencil, straight edge, and this time you might need a protractor and/or French curve.)
Let's now say you want to draw something different
than a straight line.

How about a cool peghead shape?
Dream it up and draw the shape that you want by hand. No extra tools
just your pencil and paper. Do it quickly. Use your dexterity.
If you do not like how it looks, do it again and again ... until you get
the cool shape that you are after. Don't focus on details here, just
quickly try different shapes until you get one that you like.
(It does not have to be outrageous. But draw something more than
simply a box peghead.)
Now that you have your idea down, you can use your ruler, protractor,
or French curve (Control Craftsmanship tools) to clean up your idea.

Next mark your tuners' location and add a logo if you like.

Look at your design.

Check the tuner positions on your faux peghead. Where will the
strings leave the tuner posts? Any weird angles? Too much stress on
the nut? Does your Design need any adjustment?

How does your design function?

Can you find a ready made guitar case for this new peghead shape, or
will you have to get custom cases made for each guitar? Can you find
material in these dimensions without having to mill it all yourself?
Thinking about Process during the Design can save a lot of mistakes
and effort (Dexterity) later on.

With this exercise, did you realize that you just used
Dexterity, Control, Process, and Design?

But not in that order, and more often than not, the work does not move in a direct 1,2,3,4 procedure.

Dexterity Craftsmanship drew your peghead shape, Design Craftsmanship looked to see how it functioned, Control Craftsmanship cleaned up the idea with rulers, and Process Craftsmanship told you what to do when.

You did the drawing quickly at first, then checked the function, and last did the completed final version.

At this point I want you to get the idea that this is a dance between all four parts. Dexterity, Control, Process and Design. They all four work together, all the time.

Design can be subjective. It is ultimately the responsibility of the artist. The point here is to keep the larger picture in mind as you design your product.

Your Design can help the Process or hinder it.

"Design is not just what it looks like and feels like.
Design is how it works."
Steve Jobs

Now that you are becoming aware of the Qualities of Craftsmanship, you might be surprised to see them popping up in unlikely places.

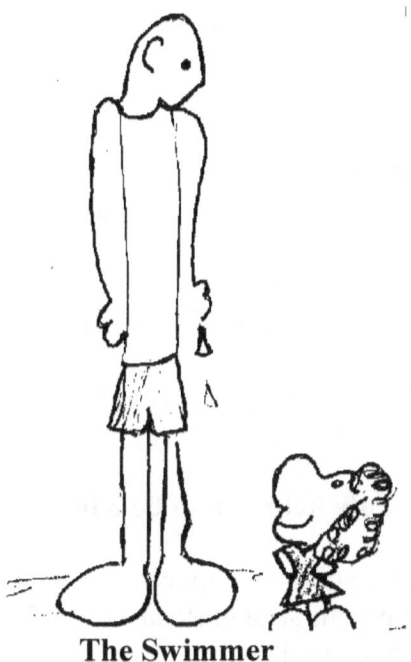

The Swimmer

Gliding through a cloud of bubbles, I was feeling pretty good about that flip turn. I nailed it. I got a strong push off the wall. All is good. I had my body angle right, and I was getting a good snap as I rotated on my axle from side to side. Hold on! Who is this passing me in the next lane? What !!!? And not just once; lap after lap I notice this person in the lane next to me just blowing me out of the water. I am a decent swimmer and usually one of the fastest in the pool. But not this time. When I finish my mile, I hop out of the water about the same time as a thin 14 year old girl climbs out of her lane.

   Wait a minute!

Standing next to her I am at least a foot taller. I am stronger and have a longer arm pull than she does, but she passed me like I was sitting still.

What is going on here? *

I enjoy swimming laps. No phone calls, just peace and quiet in my own little aquatic world. It is challenging. For me, I find it interesting, because a swimmer is always trying to improve. It's thoughtful. You are not just looking at that line on the bottom of the pool, instead one thinks about how the hand travels through the water, the body and head angles, breathing, glide, …

How does a fair swimmer become a good swimmer? What do you think? Swim ten thousand laps? Twenty thousand?

No grasshopper. If you poorly swim ten thousand laps, all you are doing is reinforcing bad habits.

It will only help you to be a better fair swimmer.

In order to become a good swimmer you need to engage your mind. Work on improving your stroke. Read the books, watch the DVDs, and get advice from a good swimming coach.

Adjust your technique, and over time you will get better.

What was I doing, and what was she doing?

I was employing Dexterity (I was moving my arms through the water) and Process. (Earlier I had taken several swimmer's stroke classes. A swimmer friend and I had recorded ourselves swimming in order to see what needed improving.)

She was using Dexterity, Control (she had hand paddles, leg buoys, a drag suit, kickboards,… to help strengthen her weak areas and to assist her in maintaining maximum use of her Dexterity – proper technique), Process (with each swim she had her coach there helping to push her to maintain a proper stroke), and Critique. (She was listening to her coach and pushing herself to follow proper Process.)

More on Critique coming in Part 2.
To my relief, it turned out that she was training for the Olympic trials.

Craftsmanship Overview – Wood Chips

- Dexterity Craftsmanship is the bottom line. It takes practice to get and is often referred to as "Eye /Hand".
Dexterity is what you want and need to develop.

- Control Craftsmanship can aid you as your Dexterity grows strength. Using jigs and templates can serve as not only training wheels while getting Dexterity,
but also as valuable tools for your Process.

- Process helps Control. This is where you will stop and think about what you are doing and when. The idea here is to move along through your process in a thoughtful purposeful manner. Do not just jump in and simply thrash around.

- Design Craftsmanship is how it works. How does your end product look and function? Did it meet your objectives? Is the Design causing you problems with the Process
or is it helping the Process?

- And last, this all works together all the time and not necessarily in sequence.

Part 2 – Implementation

"It's kind of fun to do the impossible."
Walt Disney

The Craftsmanship of Critique

No one likes to be criticized.

The word itself makes us bristle. We learned this response from childhood. This is unfortunate, because criticism is one of the most valuable tools we have, and it is free.

I spoke with many friends (artists, writers, musicians, and other guitar builders) in putting this little book together. I asked all the same question. What personality traits did they see in common with the top craftsmen that they each know? Like me, they really did not notice any consistent attributes that ran through the top workers they respected, employed, or worked with.

A neat or sloppy work space can produce a great finished product (more on this coming). A heavy drinker or stone cold sober, reliable or unreliable, friendly or mean, … all types can find "The Zone" and create exceptional work.

I am not saying all types are people you would want to do business with, but what I am talking about here is finding the ability to focus on and create something exceptional.

What does seem to be common is the ability to self critique honestly and to be able to use that critique to advantage.

Some people naturally handle it better than others, and some naturally respond poorly. There <u>does</u> seem to be a correlation between those who do excellent work and how they handle critique. So if you don't like criticism, and shut down when it is coming your way, get over it.

I have worked many guitar shows through a handful of decades, and I don't think there has been a single part of my work that has been left untouched by criticism.

The art here is to respond kindly to the idiots while waiting on the savant.

From top to bottom, I have had to endure some really snide remarks. Some of it just ridiculous, *"Hey buddy, what the hell is that; someone put some chewing gum in your guitar?"* (referring to the wax seal I use on my label), some of it uneducated, *"Why don't you build a nice looking guitar like a good ol' Gibson at half the cost?",* and finally, some of it helpful, *"I don't like to feel the sharp edges of the nut when I am playing. Most guitars have these sharp nut corners like your guitar, but I really like it when I feel a guitar that has a nut with a softer edge. That says to me that the builder is in tune with the player."* Bingo! How great is that! No middle man. Just me and the customer talking about how to make a guitar better. Suffer the good with the bad and see what great stuff you get out of it.

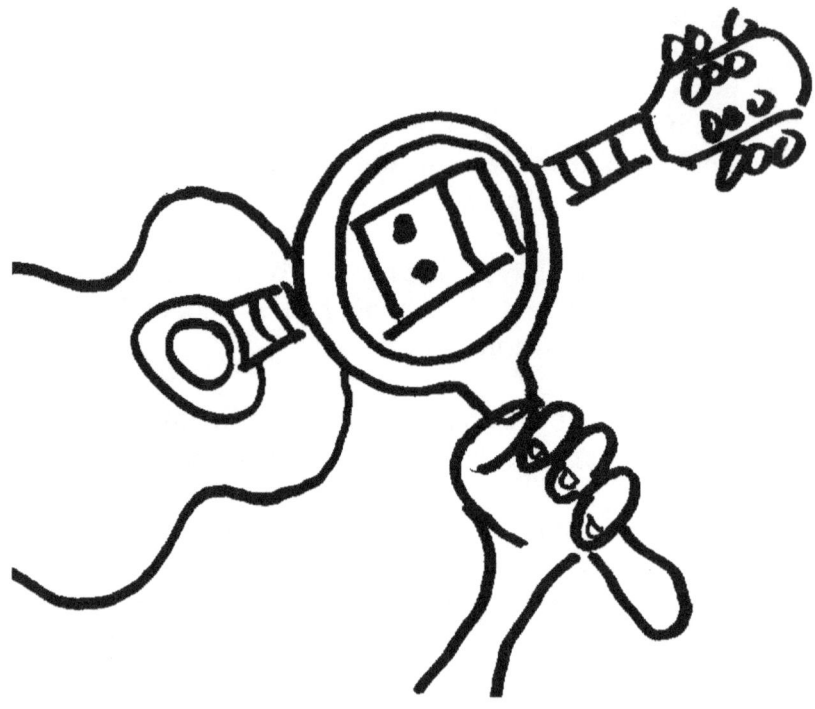

We all have a hard time honestly seeing and hearing ourselves. Hearing and seeing things in a new way is very important to the craftsman's development. It is worth investigating.

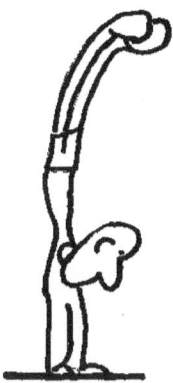

<u>The Gymnast</u>

In my youth I was a gymnast. I was too small for football, not really interested in baseball, and in my school that left a choice between either soccer or gymnastics. I worked hard at gymnastics and found my adolescent social group.

I also found life lessons that I still carry with me today.

When you learn a new trick, you read about it, see it, have it demonstrated to you, … but at some point you have to simply 'go for it'. The coach might say, "Well …you landed on your butt, because you did not keep your right arm tucked in. Let's try it again."
So second, third, fourth time, … butt, butt, butt.

And you keep saying and thinking, "But coach I AM keeping my right arm in."
Until you see the video replay of your arm flopping away from your body. At this point the good gymnast will focus on new unused muscles and keep that damn arm in. What do you know? He lands on his feet. Maybe a little wobbly at first, but this will be the tactile start of getting the trick.

He was able to see and feel something he had
 not been able to before.

Swimmers, tennis players, golfers, … we all have a hard time seeing ourselves, but it is very important.

If you keep doing it the same way that you think "feels" right, over and over, and keep getting that same crummy result, then at some point you might just give up.

This is common. A better approach would be to attack the problem from another angle.

In gymnastics, often one will have success when he can make the body move in unnatural or uncomfortable ways. Counter – intuitive. But soon this will become familiar and become the natural approach to performing the trick. I am here to tell you, at first it can feel really crazy.

Want to do a back flip? Jump up and follow your natural instinct to throw your head back. See what happens. *(Don't actually do this. You might hurt yourself.)* You will probably land flat on your back or neck. But if you jump straight up, do not throw your head back and simply raise your knees to your chest. What do you know? You flip around and land on your feet. Who would naturally try this? It seems crazy. This is where the third person comes in. Your teacher. *(I have to say that in learning this kind of trick, it is very important to have a helper to spot you. We used to start on the trampoline in a harness, then move to the floor - but not until we have first established the tactile feel of the trick. Don't try this yourself without help!)*

If you perform a step in the guitar building process and it screws up, you can say, "but coach, I had a sharp chisel. I used a nice clean piece of wood, I let it soak 5 minutes, I thinned it to .090, … I did everything I was supposed to, step by step." Again and again, you have the same unpleasant result. What has felt right to you has not been working; has it? Perhaps it is time to try something new.

Like the gymnast, it is time to step back and have a look.

You need to see something that you have not seen before.

Can you see the problem yourself?

This might be hard at first. Can you get your mind off the problem and approach it with fresh eyes? A new angle. You might be able to solve the problem by changing Process or Control Craftsmanship - revising a jig, template, or sequence.

If you are truly stuck, it might actually take getting advice from a coach (teacher) to get past this current hurtle. Working with a talented craftsman can shave a lot of effort off your learning curve. Even if it is only for an hour, day, or week at a time, grab some live classes and get better. I tell my students that a week class can shave anywhere from 10 to 20 guitars off the learning curve. It all depends on where the student is at the time and how much they can absorb. Many of my students take my classes several times and learn different things each time. The material is the same.
What changes is the student's widening ability to hear, see, and feel.

Education and guidance can play an important role in the craftsmanship dance.

In order to improve, we must learn to hear, feel, and see things that we have not been able to before.

A big step in performing music or learning a second language is learning to hear yourself. Using a recorder for playback is perfect for this. You might say, *"I did not know I was cutting off the pronunciation of that last word. Man; it certainly would sound better if I just held that chord a little longer. Who knew?"*

But if one does not stop and learn to listen, these improvements might never take place.

I bet you have had this experience while recording the message on your voice mail.

"Hello, please leave me a message, and I will call you back."

It seems pretty simple, until you have redone it 5 times
to get an acceptable message.
What do you know? You have been applying the Craftsmanship of
Critique to your voicemail!

**Make an honest assessment of your skills and
look for ways to polish the end product.**

The famous Einstein quote paraphrased, *"Insanity is when you keep
performing the same action over and over again expecting
to get a different result."*

Rembrandt is said to have looked at his work in a mirror
in order to get a fresh perspective.

So here I go, name dropping.
If these guys were on to something, maybe you can be too.

Get a fresh perspective on your work.

Example – Point of View

I used to supply 30 guitar stores across the country. It was not easy,
and I spent what little spare time I had visiting as many as I could in
order to do a little PR. Once while I was working the winter NAMM
show in Anaheim, I decided to grab a taxi to visit McCabes Music in
Santa Monica. It is just a fantastic music store, and I was delighted to
have my guitars represented there.

The manager kindly asked, "Would you mind beveling your sound
holes?" I almost jumped for joy. "Of course. That is so easy, and if
that is something your customers look for …, I am happy to do it."
I had been leaving the sound holes crisp, because I like a sharp
controlled look in my work. But to them it looked like it had not been
refined, completed. How could I have seen that change, unless he had
pointed it out? Would I have continued to be sold out at McCabes,
with nearly a two year wait, if I had not beveled the sound holes?

I saw something I had not seen before. My point of view shifted.

When we can accept critique from ourselves and from others, new unforeseen doors will open.

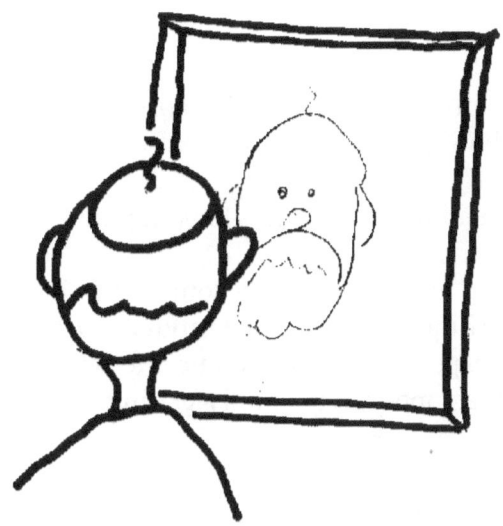

Tip - Self Critique

With every batch of guitars that I complete, I grade each instrument with a color coded chart. From top to bottom I assess each instrument. I want to see them one last time, in a different way, before they head off to their new homes.

I have a fresh look at the nut fit, peghead shape, tuner alignment, neck pitch, inlays, neck fit, rosette, binding… the whole thing.

And I mark my chart with colored pens. Green is good, yellow is fair, and red means something went wrong.

Of course I shoot for all green. Occasionally yellow shows itself, it happens. But if I see a red popping up through several guitars on the chart, I will know there is a problem with the Process, and it needs attention.

If the back brace fitting through the kerfing is chipped on a few successive instruments, I know I need to have a look at it. It might be as simple as a dull bit. Or there might be a procedural problem …whatever. It needs attention. I know it was not a one time fluke.

This is a great chart for having a look at what is going right, but the real value here is seeing what is going wrong.

To this day I am my harshest critic, because I care about my work. I bet you care about your quality too.

Stop, step back, and have an honest look at your own work.

A wonderful thing is if you can find someone (whose workmanship you admire) to critique your finished product. Offer to pay. This shows that you respect your critic's time. He will be encouraged to try to honestly help, as opposed to simply getting you out of his workshop asap.

ESL

For years I have taught an ESL class at our local library. I do it simply to offer some volunteer work. I speak Spanish and know some of the problems an adult can have in learning a second language. One of my classes involves accent reduction. We usually all sit around the table, and I ask, *"Who wants to reduce their accent?"* Twenty hands shoot up. So I say *"Well there are two ways to do it: the easy way and the hard way. Who wants the easy way?"* About fifteen hands raise, the others sense something is up. The easy way is to really want to reduce your accent. That is what most people do. They really, really want to reduce their accent, but actually do nothing about it - other than continue to really want to reduce their accent.
The problem is that way does not work.
Eye rolling from the group.
Then I get into how to listen to the rhythm of the language, focus on the vowels, record themselves, word exercises, pronunciation tricks, …
They need to learn to hear themselves.

Now who wants to improve their guitar's quality the easy way?

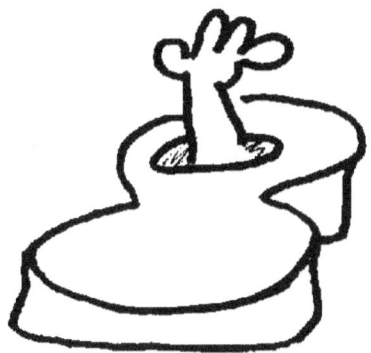

Tip –Post It Notes
In my workshop on any given day, you can walk around and see masking tape or post-its full of notes adorning my work stations. I am employing a bit of time travel here and writing notes to my future self for the next time I approach this tool.

I may be making neck blanks and during the process it occurs to me that I can cut the center laminate a half inch lower than the finger board gluing surface. After the blank is glued up, I will already have a start on the routing for the truss rod slot. There will be less wood to route and less dust to breath. All I have to do is add this small step to Process Craftsmanship.

This might occur to me after spending a day gluing neck blanks, but in a few months when I come back to this task, … well let's just say it is a good idea to make notes.

Often you can see my taped notes on various jigs throughout the shop. So when I pick that particular jig up to use, I will remember what I had learned the last time I used it.

I get better all the time.

**An honest personal critique can have a
very positive effect on your Craftsmanship.**

The Red Flags
(for luthiers)

The customer is looking for problems with your guitar and, in a way, hoping to see something that will let him "off the hook", so that he does not have to buy it.

It's a great guitar. He should have it, so don't leave him with a reason for not getting it.

At the end of my 6 day guitar building class, we, as a class, sit around and marvel at the great guitar that we have just built. After patting ourselves on the back and talking about how wonderful we all are, I like to go over the "Red Flag List".

This is an assessment of our class guitar from top to bottom while I hold the guitar on my knee.
These are the key construction points that most of us look for when judging a guitar.

This will give you an idea of what to look for when critiquing your own guitars and when looking at others. Nobody is perfect and no factory is perfect. I don't look for perfection, and you should not either.
Look for nice clean workmanship, attention to detail, a balanced aesthetic, and a consistency through the piece that bodes quality.

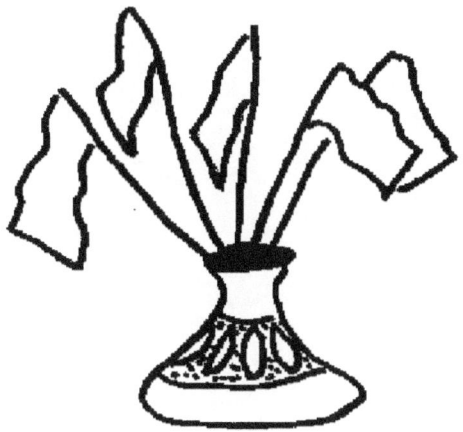

The Red Flag List

exterior

- Balanced peghead shape and even thickness
- Tuners aligned evenly
- Nice clean nut fit
- Properly dressed fingerboard – no 14th fret hump
- Fingerboard inlays inlaid tightly – not a lot of fill
- Clean fret work – no gaps under frets
- Nice tall fret crown – no scratches
- Side position markers on fingerboard follow a straight line – not a wavy line
- Fret ends beveled consistently and cleanly
- No fill at neck joint
- Nice delicate neck heel shape
- Neck fitted to center line of back and top
- Body shape - Even waist - same location on both sides
- No wavy sides – the upper and lower bout humps align looking down the sides and no flat spots
- Binding even - in depth and thickness all the way around
- No binding fill
- No chips in top around rosette or purfling around body
- Top and back domes (curvatures) even / controlled
- Bridge alignment on top - not angled or off center
- Strings align evenly over the sound hole and rosette
- Proper neck pitch for type of instrument. Room in saddle height for natural settling and action adjustment

interior

- No scratches heavier than 180 on back or sides
- <u>Bracing coming from kerfing</u> – nice tight fit
- <u>Even kerfing as it goes around the sides</u> – not a tall and short line as it goes around the body
- <u>No glue squeeze out or gaps in bracing or kerfing, etc.</u>
- <u>Clean well fitted end blocks</u>

general workmanship

- Clean sharp edges – not rounded and undefined
- Purposeful lines
- No sanding scratches
- No patch work
- Overall balance in aesthetics both in design and wood combinations

No excuses. None of this : *"It was getting late. The wood cracked after I had it glued. The clamp slipped ..."* Your customer does not care about the cat jumping on the workbench. Blah, blah, blah ... , don't bother.

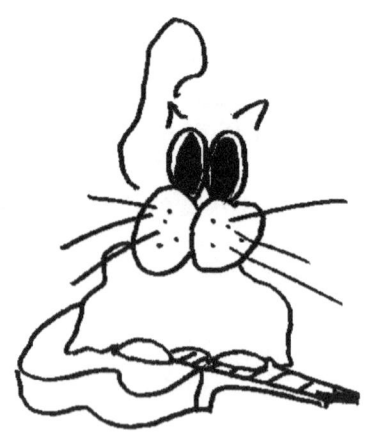

Craftsmanship of Critique – Wood Chips

- Learn to accept criticism as your friend.
  *This one thing can help you grow as
  a craftsman unlike any other.*

- Learn to remove your ego and have an honest look at your own work.

- Learn how to look at an instrument via the Red Flag List.

- Don't Make Excuses.

Your Interior Craftsman – The Magic Zone

Finding **"The Zone"** is often associated with sports.

The golfer sends a ball 300 yards and it magically lands on a patch of grass the size of a postage stamp. Meanwhile you are at home swiping away at the damn thing.

The Olympic gymnast nails the routine while her competitor misses the bar and stumbles by a millimeter.

The baseball player drops his bat as he has just struck out, when only 2 days ago he hit 3 home runs.

The professional athlete knows that the line between success and failure is quite fine. It steps us into the mystical subconscious realm of auto response.

Let's look at the baseball player's fastball.

No human being can process the speed of a fastball quickly enough to actually be able to hit it. What!!!

A fast ball from Nolan Ryan, clocked at 100.9 mph, from the pitcher's mound to the catcher's mitt takes only 0.4 seconds to arrive. The batter is faced with seeing the ball, sending the signals to the brain, contracting the muscles in order to hit the ball, and actually going for it. Amazingly this entire sequence must take less than 0.4 second. Otherwise no one would ever hit the ball.

But what is outrageous is the conscious awareness takes longer than that – about 0.5 seconds.

So … the ball travels too fast for the batter to be consciously aware of it.

(More on this type of thing and this specific study can be found in the wonderful book - Incognito by David Eagleman)

It all takes place on a subconscious level. The Zone.

A great swimmer, gymnast, guitar player, craftsman will find it difficult to actually explain how they 'do it' when they are in the zone. The act of stopping and thinking about it actually pulls them out of it.

Bob Hope was famous for asking his golfing companion if he exhaled or inhaled on his back swing. Man! That will screw you up, snapping you out of **The Zone**.

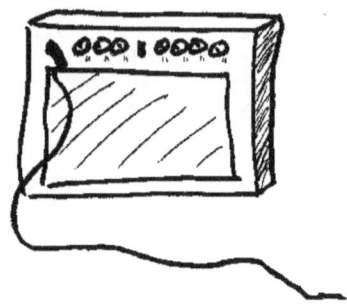

The Repair Shop
As I mentioned earlier, we had a great guitar shop in Atlanta during the 1980s. We had the talent, the location, the cool guitars, and the clients. It was really a fabulous place to work, and looking back I see that I could not have had a better place to spend my youth. One of the things that made the sixty hour work week fly by was the many talented and quirky players that would stop by. Once I had a well known customer / friend stop by my bench to say hello and to check out my current electric guitar. He took the guitar down off the wall, worked with the knobs on the crummy little shop amp, then proceeded to make the world stand still. He took the entire shop soaring with his killer pedal steel licks followed by wonderfully arpeggiated jazz floating up and down the neck. After about fifteen minutes he looks at his watch and says "What fun! Gotta go." He hangs the guitar gently back on the wall, hops onto the tour bus, and off he goes. Man I love my job.

After the shop starts getting back to the daily work of setups and fret jobs, I gently take the guitar from the wall and plug it into the amp. I made sure not to even breathe on a single knob. All I can say is, the magic walked out the door. The cool part was in his fingertips, not the amp set up or the guitar.

He knew how to step in and out of the Zone. He did it every time he played.

You have been there too. Ever read a book or played a video game and pop your head up to see that it has gotten dark outside? You then realize that you are hungry. You were in "The Zone".

When your focus is so astute that the surrounding world ceases to exist, that is it.

The batting coach can help the batter improve the odds of hitting the ball. Hand and feet placement, breathing, smooth swing, ... The difference between the major leaguer who is clobbering the ball out of the park and the guy who consistently can only get a single is very little. Both work the same amount of time in the batting cage, both have access to the same coaches, weight training, guidance,... But one has a better connection to "it" than the other.

More home runs lead to more home runs. More first base hits lead to more base hits. It is funny how the brain works and sets up patterns - successful patterns or not so successful ones.

Occasional success can take you to frequent success. Frequent success will lead you to skill.

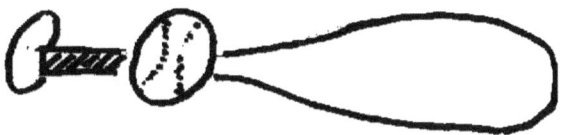

7 Things to Help Your Batting Average

What I can do here is help you to create a better
environment for finding **"The Zone"**.

Let's find some occasional success together, and that can nudge
you towards frequent success, and before too long
- look out - you will have skill.

1) The Goal

Envision the job beforehand.
Plan out the steps you will be taking and what tools you will be using.
See the killer end product – that beautiful guitar sounding great on the
knee of the happy customer. This is really fun and is usually
accompanied by lying awake in bed at night with a wiggling foot.

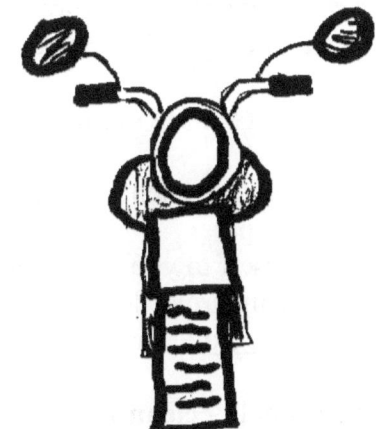

Example - Motorcycle Riding
This is a curious thing, but when gliding along on a motorcycle,
if you look at the pot hole, you will hit the pot hole. All riding
improvement and sport riding books mention this. What one quickly
learns to do is to see the pot hole, then look past
it to where you want the bike to go.

Now that is a good analogy.

2) Work Environment

Nothing can snap you out of the Zone faster than being interrupted by a phone call. You use one part of your brain for carving a guitar neck and a completely different area of the brain gets used for talking on the phone. Moving back and forth between these mental functions is going to screw you up. Create a situation where you do only one thing at a time. Focus.

(More on this in How to Make a Living Doing Something Crazy.)

If you want to find the Zone, you must create an environment where you can utilize only one part of the brain at a time. Focus.

"Honey, please do not interrupt me for the next hour, unless the house is on fire" are magic words. And turn the damn phone off! This simple advice can make a big difference.

Be neat.

I have worked with several very talented craftsmen who were slobs. This is not for you grasshopper.
If you want to present yourself to your customer as a quality act - **clean up**. Walking around in circles looking for a tool will kill your flow and snap you out of the Zone - **clean up**.

If you want to avoid accidents - **clean up**.

In my shop rule number one is:
"You are not done, until you have **cleaned up**".
It is so much nicer to come into your workshop at the beginning of the day if it looks nice and is neat. I do not mean that you must vacuum and put all the tools away every time you leave your shop. What I suggest is take 5 minutes and pick up the loose paper towels and garbage, arrange the tools and work neatly on the bench, sweep up the big stuff,… **clean up your act**.

This is where you are spending your life, why not make it nice?

3) Practice

This book is a complete waste of time, both for you to read and for me to write, unless you spend time in your shop.

Practice. You will need to have a tactile experience at least a few times per week in order to improve. Like most of my contemporaries, I have put in decades of 60 hour weeks. But this might not be reasonable in your case. Even so, if you want to improve as a craftsman, you will need to spend consistent time in the shop. Maybe 2 hours every Monday, Wednesday, and Friday night. Figure it out, and schedule yourself some regular shop time.
2 hours every 2 weeks will not do it.
There is a momentum that gets developed by regular shop time.
It multiplies every week.

I imagine that for me, my hour in the shop is much more powerful than your hour in the shop.
I have quite a 'head of steam' built up.

If you have to restart your cold engine every time, your learning curve will be lower and your success will come slower.

**Dedicate yourself to regular shop time
and watch yourself improve.**

Thoughtful Progress.

You cannot develop a feel for the tool or process without practice. In order to refine your time behind the workbench, think about what you are doing. Think of ways to improve. (Remember all the little notes I have written to myself decorating my workshop?)
Like swimming laps, paying attention is really the only way to get better.

Tip: Having a problem with patience? Is frustration taking hold of you and pulling you out of the Zone? Set a workshop time of 1.5 hours then stop. Step away from your work, and tomorrow see how it is going. Sometimes setting a fixed amount of shop time can help the student achieve patience, learn not to rush the work, and maintain control.

If you lack Patience try substituting Self Discipline.
You can create a good work ethic via habit.

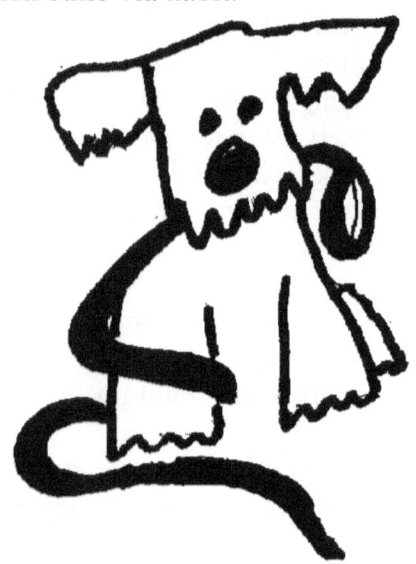

Example Joey
I walk with my buddy Joey everyday. Rain or shine, we are out there trodding along. He is a great little dog and really smart. When I was training him to heel, he often would get distracted, too excited, and start pulling on the leash, almost as if he wanted to get under those cars roaring by.

When he forgot to heel, I would simply stop
and wait for him to get his focus back.

You can do this too.

**Sometimes the best tool that you have at your disposal
is a walk around the block.**

4) Attitude

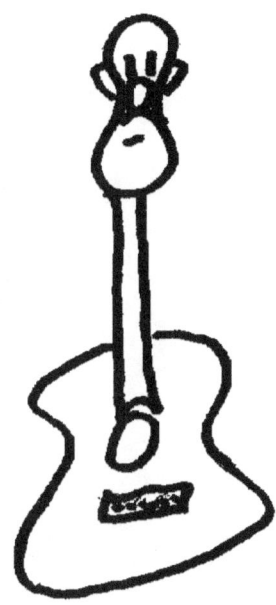

You are not your guitar.

Avoid equating your self worth with the project
sitting on your workbench.

Forget public opinion.

**Failure is not the opposite of success, it is an element of success.
It is a step towards success.**

Stop taking ownership of the problem. You can take responsibility for
it, but a stupid problem does not mean you are a bad or untalented
person. Visit any workshop, and you will notice a lot of parts, gone
wrong, lying around.

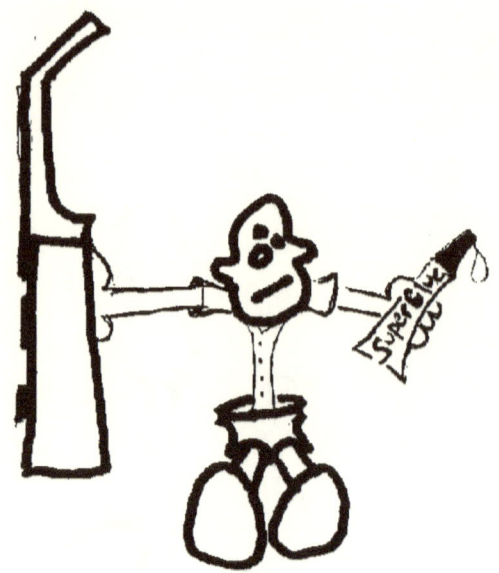

Example – Bad glue

Let's say you glued a bridge on a guitar and a month later it is pulling off. You know the guitar was maintained in a proper environment.

   Your response is:
a) Damn it, the glue did not hold. Why me?
b) Damn it, the glue did not hold, I thought it looked funny when it came out of the bottle. Next time I will not use it if it looks even a little weird.

Workman A is blaming the glue for the problem.

Craftsman B is accepting responsibility.

Which one are you?

5) Details –

I hope you choose to dedicate yourself to doing your best,
all the time.
If so, focus on the details. Even aspects of the project that are hidden
from view are done well. This is more of a philosophy
than a hard fast rule.
I strongly believe that you cannot turn quality on and off.
You either do good work or you do not. You either try to play the
guitar well every time you pick it up, or you simply hope that you will
be able to play well when you need to. It is either an "all the time" or
"hope for the best" type of situation.
I am not suggesting that you apply the same level of detail to
remodeling your bathroom as you do to building a guitar. This is
misplaced energy. You would never get done with that tile work and
you would be completely exhausted every day.
What I am suggesting is that you make the choice. You are in control,
and you make the reasonable decisions.
This is Craftsmanship.

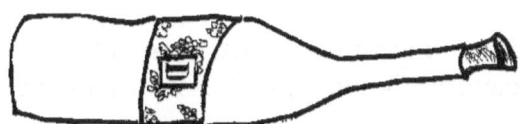

Example – Wine

I have a buddy who is a wine connoisseur. We were talking about
why some wine is really good and others fantastic. What makes the
difference? His response, "Everyone does the same big things in
pretty much the same way. The ones that get "it" sweat the small
stuff: soil, annual rain, type of rain (forest fire = smoky rain = unique
flavor), climate and temperature effects on the life of the grape,…
the organic parts really matter."

Whether it is a part of the guitar or a unique grape,
the magic can be found in the details.

This is the kind of thing Steve Jobs was crazy for. He pushed his company to make all the parts of his product look good, even the parts that no customer would ever see. He believed that all of it affected the end product.

Sam Maloof was kidded once about sanding the bottom of a drawer that no one would ever see, "But I know it is there."

Here is my approach to building a guitar :

I look at it as a conglomeration of many little art projects.

I am not waiting for the big emotional reward at the end.
I don't think that would be any fun.

The nut - fitted properly, polished, height and spacing correct, no sharp edges, … that is a work of art.

The rosette - nice color, cool design, no chips, flows into the end of the fingerboard …that is a work of art.

The binding – nice miter joints, even in thickness and height, beautiful figure, … that is a work of art.

I enjoy myself the entire trip.

6) Rules

Why not have a board meeting with yourself and make some guidelines to work by? When stuck in a sticky situation, you can refer to the deal that you made with yourself (prior to being in trouble) for guidance

5 Examples

1) I want to build the best guitars, and I want my customers to enjoy them.

2) If I feel off, tired, grumpy ... I will walk away and watch it magically come into focus later.
(I do not know why this is so hard to learn, but it works.)

3) I will keep my shop clean, so that I don't slip in the dust, catch my balance by putting my hand down on the spinning table saw blade. (I saw it happen.)

4) I will keep Optimism as my guiding principle

5) I will do the absolute best I can right now, even though I know the next guitar will always be better.

Have a chat with yourself and <u>make your own list</u>.

7) Standardize

Consider this: If each of your guitar tops has a different rosette and every guitar body has a different thickness of binding, you will be adding to your need for Dexterity Craftsmanship.

Even if you are using Control Craftsmanship to do the task (binding cutter), you will be using Dexterity Craftsmanship to set up the bit's depth, width,… each time for a different thickness and width.

If all your guitars have the same rosette and binding dimensions, your need for Dexterity Craftsmanship lowers, and you will be able to rely more on the Control side of things.

I am not saying to standardize all your instruments.

What I am saying is this is an example of how all the systems fit together. This is simply something for you to become aware of as your skills develop.

You can use many different kinds of binding material, but why not make them all the same dimensions? It certainly makes life easier.

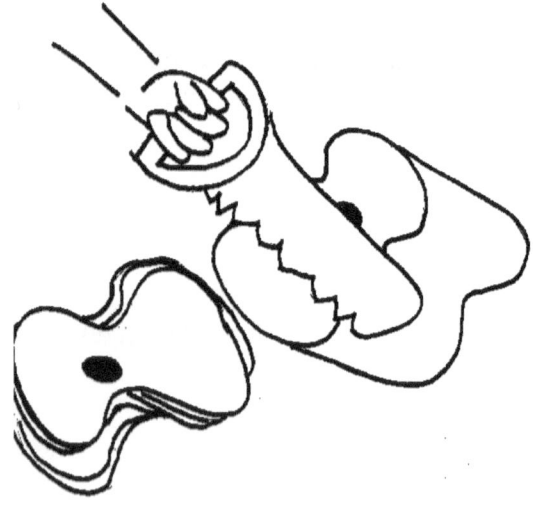

The Zone Woodchips

- **The Zone happens on a subconscious level**

- **You can build frequent success with occasional success**

- **7 things to help you create a healthy environment for the Zone**

- **Make your own rules as a Guideline to work by**

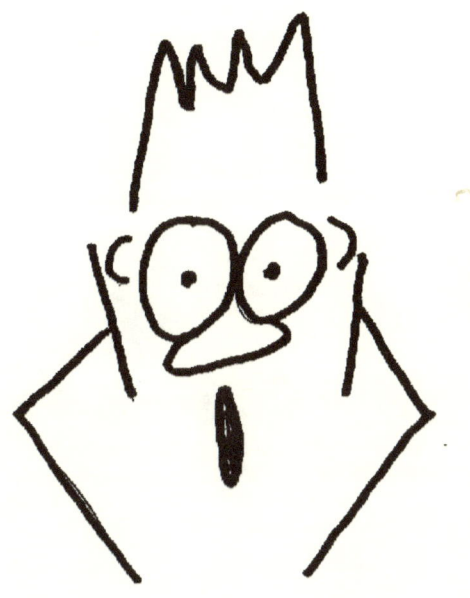

Failure

Critique, Failure,…. What kind of book is this anyway?

"If you want to live your life in a creative way, as an artist, you have to not look back too much."
Steve Jobs

The student is standing there with head hung down and feeling pretty bad about himself. This is the familiar posture after a mistake or error. And usually it is a real whopper. I will walk over and pat him on the back and say, *"It happens. I don't think you can do anything that I have not done myself."*

Until you have royally messed up every part of the guitar during the building process, you really do not know how to build a guitar.

Until you crash, you do not know where the edge of the envelope is or how lucky you had been up to that point.

When I say this to one of my long time guitar builder friends, it is usually met with a nodding head and knowing smile.

This failure conundrum makes for a bitter sweet experience.
The sweet is the enormous amount of information you get that will prepare you for the next time. The encouraging thing here is, the failures get smaller.

"A craftsman is someone who can hide his mistakes well."

I hate that saying. Hate it!

That phrase does not give credit to the Craftsman.

The Craftsman makes smaller mistakes.

Look at the failure as a prototype.
It is not the opposite of success but a step towards success.
I know I said this earlier, but come on, it's great. Isn't it?
I want to bang you knuckleheads over the head with this concept.

I recently read an article about problems with
teenage children that applies here.

"As teenagers, most of us do stupid things while we figure out
how to be smarter."

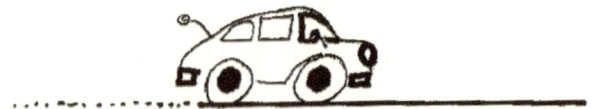

In my life my windshield is a lot larger
than my rear view mirror.

I am always planning the next fun project or design.

As I was developing my own guitar building Process, I traveled the country to promote my instruments and to visit guitar productions.

I came away with 3 comforting things:

1) - I was on the right track. I saw that the luthiers, who I admired, built their guitars (on a larger scale) in a very similar manner that I used for mine.

2) - Most of the tooling they use is accessible to me. I saw how I could make similar jigs using fairly simple tooling.

3) - They made mistakes too. Big ones. In any given guitar shop, whoever it is, you will see guitar bodies and necks that did not make it through to the end.

That certainly made me feel better,
and it should make you feel better too.

You are going to screw up.

That's life.

Get over it.

Sometimes the craftsman can take a bitter failure and turn it into a success. You might think that you will never get a return on the effort, but you will in terms of knowledge and experience. This is the valuable stuff.

"Nobody tells this to people who are beginners. I wish someone had told me. All of us who do creative work, we get into it because we have good taste. But there is this gap. For the first couple of years you make stuff, it is just not that good. It is trying to be good, it has potential, but it is not. But your taste, the thing that got you into the game, is still killer. And if you are just starting out or you are still in this phase, you gotta know that it's normal and the most important thing you can do is do a lot of work. Put yourself on a deadline so that every week you finish a piece. It is only by going through a volume of work that you will close that gap, and your work will be as good as your ambitions. And I took longer to figure out how to do this than anyone I've ever met. It's gonna take a while. It is normal to take awhile. You just gotta fight your way through."

Ira Glass

7 TSMs

Typical Student Mistakes

During my Advanced Guitar Building Workshop,
I throw out to the class TSMs
as we go through the week building a guitar together.

Here are a few things to avoid as your craftsmanship develops.

1) Man, look at all these cool tools that I have!

Right off the student tends to run out and buy the best Marpel chisels, Delta bandsaw, a fleet of Porter Cable routers, …
And they often build complicated motorized radius disk sanding devices, extravagant go-bar decks, and on and on… This is major overkill. And it is killing your inner craftsman.

Keep your tooling simple and get started building a guitar.

Taking the common "over tooling route", often the student never gets down to actually building the guitar. He has created a lot of pressure for himself by buying all this stuff. Now he not only has to build a guitar, but he has to build a great guitar.

I built my first 30 guitars with a 12" bandsaw, a dremel, and a table sander. (This was prior to being able to buy pre-dimensioned wood, so I hired a large cabinet shop to re-saw my lumber I found at a local cabinet supply shop, and I used to thickness the wood largely by hand plane.)

You can do a little better than my meager budget allowed in 1977, but do not fall prey to the temptation to overdo it.

**Tip - Particle board and dry wall screws first,
  Baltic birch plywood and threaded brass inserts later.**

Why put all the effort into building a beautiful finished jig before knowing the thing is really going to work? And even if it does work, you will continue to see ways to improve it after using it a few times. (At least I hope so.) So I suggest particle board and dry wall screws for the working first edition.
By not being married to it, via the amount of time and money put into it, you will be quicker to toss it and build the new improved version 2.0.

Only later take the time to make that nice looking jig or template.

**Keep it simple - at first.
Your odds of success go way up if you do.**

2) I use only the best Brazilian. I have to.

Oh no you don't. The student wants to build the best guitar that he can. Good! So again he adds needless pressure on himself by buying the most expensive German spruce and the most beautiful Brazilian Rosewood that he can find.
"Now I cannot screw up. I really have to be careful!"

This is crazy! Give yourself a break and build the first few with good old Indian rosewood or Mahogany and Sitka spruce.
It is still going to be a great guitar.
Why make things harder on yourself? Remember you are going to mess up. Everyone does. Life happens.

Why not save our earth's precious resources (and your money) until you have begun to make those mistakes smaller mistakes?

3) Let's throw some more pearl work on it.

Often the student is thrilled by adding lots
of appointments to his first guitar –
Heavy inlay work, armbevel, soundport, carvings, all the bells and
whistles that he has seen on other guitars …
But the truth is, you will not be able to hide your poor
workmanship with 'bling'.
 Don't even try; it looks foolish.
 Instead focus on controlled execution.
 The 'bling' can wait. It's not going anywhere.

4) Perfection

The student shoots for perfection. And sadly when something
does go wrong, he will shelf the guitar never to return.

Allow yourself a learning curve.
Apply the principles that you are learning here, and be careful. It
will be a good guitar.

**Grasshopper keep in mind, you are a grasshopper.
You will screw up.**

So plan on it, learn from it, and move ahead to the next one.

These unrealistic expectations, that the beginner arrives with, are the
guards at the gate that are keeping you from improving and,
more importantly, enjoying yourself.

Ego, money, criticism, lack of skill, lack of patience, poor influences
(even though you can learn a lot from bad examples), poor
environment, arrogance, lack of training…they are not your friends.
Don't let this foolishness keep you from your goal.

5) I'll get back to it.

There is much lost by not completing your first guitar. You have
passed up on a lot of knowledge that is sitting there waiting for you.
So you made a mistake. Big deal. I make them all the time.
Do not miss this opportunity to learn.
You have to let go to complete the project. You can learn about
binding, frets, bridges, bending sides, … all the individual
components that go into your guitar. But you cannot learn about
completing the guitar until it is making music on your knee.

Finish the damn thing!

Even if it is not that great masterpiece that you had in mind when you
first started, it still is wonderful. You were able to actually build
a guitar. Congrats. Be happy.

6) The Better Mouse Trap Awaits.
The student reads all the books, watches all the DVDs and You Tube
clips, and improves on the 'tried and true' before even trying the
'tried and true'. Making the better mouse trap can be a lot of fun. It is
tempting, engaging, and addictive.
 And there is nothing wrong with it.
But it can impede your development as a craftsman.
Choose a clean construction technique and follow it. Later you can
improvise to your heart's content, but …

Develop skill first, or skill might never arrive.

7) Is it a Table or a Guitar?

The student will often overbuild the guitar, because he does not know the cut off points. So "Better safe than sorry"
is the prevailing motto.
I understand this. It can be really intimidating being by yourself in your workshop, especially when you are doing something as complicated as building a guitar.
 I have no sage advice for this.

The best thing is to take a class, so you can experience the build with the guidance of an experienced teacher. If that is not possible, follow, as closely as possible, the measurements given with whatever construction method you choose. Be as precise as you can be, and you can get a very good result.

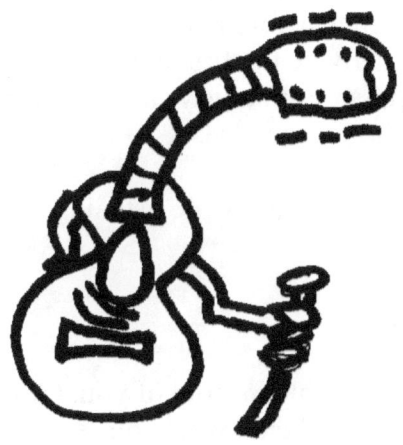

One of our class discussion topics is, "How long do you want this guitar to last?" 10 years, 30 years, 50 years, 100 years, 200 years?

Personally, I am not building guitars so they will sound good for my grandkids. I want them to be great today.

But then again, I know where the edge of the envelope is.
You will learn it too.

Al Fin –Use your Noggin
Alas, our time together is almost through.

Here are two final exercises that will help to open your awareness, change your point of view, and help you put that eight pound lunk floating in your skull to use.

Exercise – Listening

This will open your ears to the art of listening. How will you know how to get that wonderful tone, if you do not know what it is that you are after? You cannot get there if you do not know where you are going. In my classes one of the "ah ha" moments is during this listening exercise. You can do this yourself at home with a friend. Get a few different guitars (all the same flavor – classical, steel string, archtop, …), have someone play the same simple chord progression on each guitar with your back turned from the guitars. Mix them up and go through this several times before revealing which guitar is which guitar. This could actually be the first time you stopped, paid attention and listened to a guitar. I am always amazed at how much the student gets out of this simple exercise.

You now have learned to pay attention while listening.
You just got better.

Exercise – See it differently.

Put a jar, glass, and flower on a table in front of you. (Any similar items are just fine.) Now quickly sketch what you see in front of you. How does it look? Good, fair, or crummy?
Now let's look at those items in a different way. Close one eye and draw the negative space between the items. Not the items themselves, but the space between the pieces. Then complete your exercise by drawing the items using the negative space lines as your guide. I bet it looks a lot better.

You learned to see the jar, glass, and flower in a different way.
You just got better.

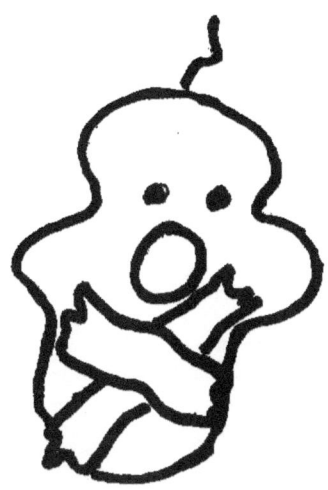

Will this guy ever shut up? OK. Here is the end.

With this new view of craftsmanship, its various components, and how they work together, you can be more thoughtful about your work.

If you engage your mind as you proceed, the work becomes three dimensional.

It is more than simply the saw and the wood. You now can watch from a different perspective, and you will notice the various qualities of craftsmanship coming together to help you.

Keep in mind that much of what we call skill is simply knowledge.

Thanks for taking the time to read my thoughts on craftsmanship. I hope you come away from this little book with fresh ideas that you can put to use - today.

Now ... go build something beautiful.

Reference Reading

Incognito - The Secret Lives of the Brain - David Eagleman

The Nature and Art of Workmanship - David Pye

~ Other Little Books by Kent Carlos Everett ~

How to make a Living Doing Something Crazy

Building Guitar Number 500

~ Instructional DVDs by Kent Carlos Everett ~

Voicing a Steel String Acoustic Guitar

Adjusting a Steel String Acoustic

The Transitional Armbevel

~ Please visit ~

www.EverettGuitars.com

&

You can follow weekly workshop activity at
Facebook / Everett Guitars

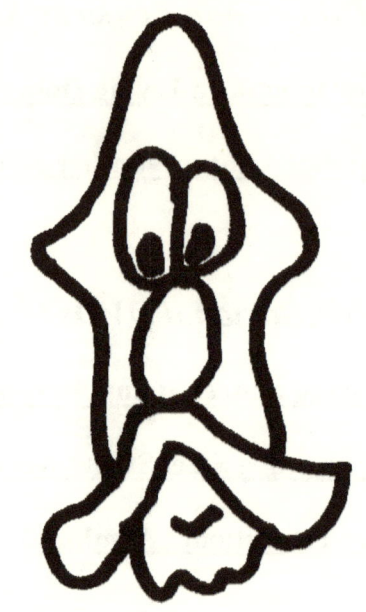

Kent Carlos Everett has not had a real job since 1977.

That was the year he built his first guitar, and he has enjoyed every minute since then in this crazy world of luthiery. Today his time is divided between building a handful of wonderful instruments each year and teaching advanced guitar building workshops from his studio in scenic north Georgia (1 hour from Atlanta).

Everett has had the pleasure of lecturing at the Healdsburg Guitar Festival, the Guild of American Luthiers Convention, the Georgia Woodworkers Guild, the Association of String Instrument Artisan's Symposium, the Southeast Bluegrass Association, as well as various schools and universities.

He has been a member of The Guild of American Luthiers since 1978 and is a founding member of the American Association of String Instrument Artisans.

His work has been exhibited in several museums including – the Museum of Making Music, the Smithsonian (the Hearts and Hands exhibit), and the Museum of Florida Craftsmen.

In print his work has been featured in Fine Woodworking's prestigious Design Books 4, 5, & 6, and on the cover of String Letter Press' Custom Guitars. Also articles about and by Everett can be read in American Lutherie, Soundboard, Acoustic Guitar, and Guitar Player magazines.

Brad Paisley, Frank Rodgers, Don Cognoscenti, David Wilcox, Bebo Norman, Amy Ray, Rich Williams, Gregg Allman, and many many others enjoy the quality of an Everett.

Everett has currently been building guitars for nearly four decades, as he says,

"I am still trying to develop the lifestyle that everyone thinks I have."

Daily concerts are given from the kitchen table for his patient wife and adoring dogs.